Robot Childminder

JONNY ZUCKER

Illustrated by Sarah McConnell

OXFORD
UNIVERSITY PRESS

OXFORD

UNIVERSITY PRESS

Great Clarendon Street, Oxford OX2 6DP

Oxford University Press is a department of the University of Oxford.
It furthers the University's objective of excellence in research, scholarship,
and education by publishing worldwide in

Oxford   New York

Auckland   Cape Town   Dar es Salaam   Hong Kong   Karachi
Kuala Lumpur   Madrid   Melbourne   Mexico City   Nairobi
New Delhi   Shanghai   Taipei   Toronto

With offices in

Argentina   Austria   Brazil   Chile   Czech Republic   France   Greece
Guatemala   Hungary   Italy   Japan   Poland   Portugal   Singapore
South Korea   Switzerland   Thailand   Turkey   Ukraine   Vietnam

Oxford is a registered trade mark of Oxford University Press
in the UK and in certain other countries

British Library Cataloguing in Publication Data
Data available

ISBN 978-0-19-911359-0

10

Available in packs
Stage 11 More Stories B Pack of 6:
ISBN 978-0-19-911353-8
Stage 11 More Stories B Class Pack:
ISBN 978-0-19-911354-5
Guided Reading Cards also available:
ISBN 978-0-19-911361-3

Printed in China by Imago

1
Metal Man

'I got the new job,' Mum grinned.
'I start next week.'

Dale and Katie cheered. Mum had really wanted this new job.

'But there's one problem,' Mum added. 'My day finishes at five o'clock. That means I can't pick you up from school and make your tea. So I've got you a childminder.'

'Who is it?' Dale asked.

'Mrs Smart from number fifty seven,' Mum said.

Dale and Katie groaned.

Mrs Smart had looked after them once before. She had a pointy nose and she was very bossy. She never, *ever* smiled.

'Can't you get someone else?' Dale begged.

'She's not that bad!' said Mum.

Dale stomped out of the kitchen. Mrs Smart was a nightmare. He and Katie did *not* want her as their childminder.

Later that night, Dale asked his mum if he could phone Grandpa for five minutes. Dale's grandpa was a famous inventor. Mum said yes.

Soon, Katie and Mum heard him talking on the phone.

Two days later, an enormous package
arrived for Dale. It was from Grandpa.
Dale wheeled it into the garden shed.
He spent the next two evenings in the
shed, banging and hammering.

On Friday night, he had a big
surprise for Mum and Katie.

Dale wheeled out a metal man.

'Meet Clarence!' Dale said. He pressed a button.

Suddenly, the metal man came to life. Two purple lights came on in his eyes. He lifted up his metal arms.

'Hello, there,' the robot said. 'My name is Clarence. How can I help you, today? Would you like me to do the school run? Or shall I run you a bath?'

Mum and Katie stared at the huge, smiling robot.

'He's our new childminder,' Dale explained. 'What do you think, Mum?'

'I … I don't know *what* to think,' she said.

'Give him a chance,' Dale begged.

'PLEASE!' said Katie.

Dale and Katie spent Saturday teaching Clarence how to do jobs round the house.

On Saturday night, they tidied up the living room.

'Wow!' said Mum. 'Maybe Clarence *is* as good as Mrs Smart.'

'So can he be our childminder?' Katie asked.

Mum smiled and then nodded.

'Yes!' cried Dale, punching the air.

Just then, the doorbell rang. It was Mrs Smart.

'When do I start?' Mrs Smart asked, bossily.

'Er – we've got this amazing robot called Clarence and – er – he's our new childminder,' Mum said. 'I'm really sorry, but we won't be needing you.'

'A robot called Clarence!' Mrs Smart cried.

'I know it sounds strange –' Mum said.

But Mrs Smart was already storming up the road. 'No robot is as good as I am!' she shouted. 'That Clarence of yours will be a disaster – you wait and see.'

2

Clarence gets busy

At school on Monday, Dale was looking forward to seeing Clarence. He'd told everyone about the robot and by the end of the day, there was a big crowd at the school gates.

But everyone was laughing at something.

Dale pushed his way through the crowd.

There was Clarence. He was wearing an enormous, purple flowery hat and a bright pink dress.

'*Where did you get that dress?*'
Dale hissed.

'A lovely woman in the street stopped
me,' Clarence beamed. 'She said I had
to wear these things to school.'

'What did she look like?' Dale asked.

'She had a pointy nose,' Clarence
replied.

'*Mrs Smart!*' Dale said to Katie, as
they hurried away from the grinning
crowd of children. 'She's trying to spoil
everything.'

By the time they got home, Dale was feeling better. It was only his first day, after all. Clarence had to learn.

'Just don't talk to the woman with the pointy nose,' he told Clarence.

Clarence nodded and took off the hat and dress.

'Go and do your homework,' Clarence said. 'I'll make your tea.'

Dale did his homework. He didn't hear the phone ringing.

Half an hour later, a burning smell wafted out from the kitchen. Dale ran downstairs. The kitchen was full of smoke. Choking and spluttering, Dale pushed open a window.

As the smoke cleared, he saw Clarence standing there.

He was smiling and holding two plates. On each plate was a pizza, some chips and some peas. They were burnt black.

'Let's eat!' cried Clarence.

'*What are you doing?*' yelled Dale.

'A woman phoned while you were doing your homework,' replied Clarence. 'I told her what I was cooking and she said I was doing it wrong. She said that food only tastes good when it's black.'

Dale groaned, grabbed the plates and scooped the burnt food into the bin. Mrs Smart again! She was ruining everything.

'Don't answer the phone!' he told Clarence and he made cheese sandwiches for himself and Katie.

When Mum came home, she sniffed the air. 'Did Clarence burn something?'

'Only a bit,' Dale said.

'OK,' Mum replied. She looked at the three of them. 'Why don't you tell me about Clarence's first day?'

3
Trolley dash

Over the next few days, the other children at school kept calling Clarence 'Metal Mum'. Dale was getting fed up with it.

On Friday afternoon, Clarence took Dale and Katie to the supermarket. Mum had given him a shopping list. Dale relaxed. What could go wrong on a simple shopping trip?

But as soon as they entered the supermarket, Clarence lifted Dale and Katie into the shopping trolley. He wouldn't let them get out.

Then he started whizzing up and down, grabbing things and throwing them on top of Dale and Katie.

'Only babies and toddlers go in trolleys!' Dale shouted.

'Not true!' cried Clarence. 'Someone e-mailed me today. They told me how to do the shopping. They said I had to put everything in the trolley.'

'Nooooo!' yelled Dale.

'*Woo hoo!*'
shouted Katie,
as Clarence
zoomed faster and
faster. Lots of children
from their school were in
the supermarket and they
were grinning and pointing.

'Metal Mum's gone mad!' one of
them shouted.

Clarence pushed them all the way
home in the trolley. Dale hid his face in
his hands. They reached the house and
Clarence swung the front door open.

But as he let go of the trolley, it crashed against the doorstep. Dale, Katie and all of the shopping flew through the air and landed on the ground. What a mess!

At that moment, Mum arrived. *'What is going on?'* she cried.

That night, Dale heard Mum on the phone.

'Thanks, Mrs Smart,' she said. 'You were right. Clarence *has* been a disaster. Can you start as soon as possible?'

Mum put the phone down and Dale said, 'I heard what you said to Mrs Smart.'

'I'm sorry, Dale,' Mum said. 'But it's no good. Clarence is a great invention but he keeps getting into trouble.'

'It's not Clarence's fault,' Dale said. 'It's Mrs Smart. She tells him to do everything wrong!'

'No, Dale,' Mum said. 'Clarence has got to go.'

'But ...'

'I've made up my mind,' said Mum, firmly.

Dale's heart sank. 'Can we have him for one more day?' he said. 'Please?'

'OK,' said Mum. '*One more day.*'

Dale and Clarence stayed up very late. They were in the shed, whispering to each other and making crashing noises.

'It's your last chance to show everyone what you can do!' Dale said to Clarence. 'So don't forget to bring my skateboard!'

4
Sparks fly!

The next day, Dale and Katie were
waiting for Clarence at the school gates.
Suddenly, Dale saw two men push a
woman over. They grabbed her bag.

'Stop!' Dale shouted. 'After them,
Clarence!'

Clarence was there in a flash. He was
carrying Dale's skateboard.

'Don't forget what I showed you last
night,' yelled Dale.

Clarence nodded, jumped onto
the board and lifted Dale and Katie up
onto his shoulders. There were lots of
kids around and they started to laugh
at Clarence. He pushed his right foot
against the ground. Sparks flew out
from his metal foot. Everyone gasped.

Clarence sped forward.

The three of them hurtled out of the
school gate, after the robbers.

Clarence scooped up two plastic dustbins and passed them up to Dale and Katie. As they overtook the robbers, Dale and Katie each dropped their bins onto a robber. The robber with the bag was so surprised that he dropped it.

Clarence screeched to a halt and placed his powerful hands on top of the bins. The robbers shouted from under the bins but there was nothing they could do.

Everyone cheered and clapped and ran over to Dale and Katie.

'A skateboarding robot!' shouted someone. 'Wow!'

Five minutes later the police arrived and led the robbers away. The woman whose bag had been stolen stepped out of a police car. Dale stopped.

He knew her.

It was Mrs Smart.

That night, Dale walked to the shed with Clarence.

'It's been amazing!' smiled Dale.

'It really has,' agreed Clarence. 'I love being your childminder.'

They said nothing for a few moments and then Dale asked sadly, 'Are you ready?'

Clarence patted Dale on the arm. 'I'm ready,' he nodded. 'I'm not going far away.'

Mrs Smart had hurt her leg when the robbers pushed her over. She couldn't walk for the next two weeks. Mum had said that maybe Clarence could help her!

Mum had asked her new boss if she could leave work early for two weeks. He said that was fine. So Mum picked Dale and Katie up after school.

They walked home past Mrs Smart's house. She was sitting in her garden.

Just then, Clarence came out of her house. He was holding a teapot.

'Do I put the teabags in the washing machine and the socks in the cup,' Clarence asked. 'Or is it the other way around?'

'He's not a disaster after all, is he?' said Mrs Smart, with a big smile. 'I'm going to miss him when he goes back to being a childminder!'

31

About the author

I once read in a newspaper
about a Japanese robot that
could do housework. This
gave me the idea for a robot
childminder. I wondered
what kind of adventures it
might have and what might
happen to the children it
was minding!

I live in north London and as well as writing
children's books, I strum my guitar, play with
my two young sons and dream of playing for
Arsenal.